This book belongs to:

_____

Contents

My secret book of rules   3

Twelve dancing princesses   19

The meeting   31

Information pullout

New words   33

*Learning to read
with this book*   35

Read with Ladybird   36

Cover illustration by Guy Parker-Rees

Published by Ladybird Books Ltd
27 Wrights Lane London W8 5TZ
A Penguin Company
3 5 7 9 10 8 6 4
© LADYBIRD BOOKS LTD MCMXCVII

Printed in Italy

My secret book of rules

written by Geraldine Taylor
illustrated by Guy Parker-Rees

Rules for my mum

Give me chocolate ice cream
six times a day and
let me keep my worm collection
in my bedroom and
let me keep my smelly socks on
all night — they're nice and warm.

Don't tell me to kiss my little sister
and don't look at me when
my dad falls on a marble ...

I didn't put it there!

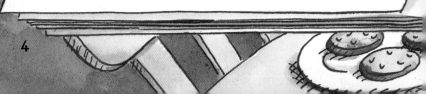

5

Rules for my dad

Don't tell me to be nice
to my little sister and
then blame me when she gets
all messy.
I am being nice to her.

Don't make me put my worms back
in the garden and don't yell,
"Keep that horrible dog away
from me!" when my dog runs in
the mud and smells.

I can't help it!

Rules for my little sister

Stop getting me into trouble with my dad.

Why can't you tell him we **are** playing nicely?

Stop smelling and please stop yelling—my ears don't like it.

Hurry up and get big enough to play football and say "thank you" when I put worms in your T-shirt.

9

Rules for my teacher

Put a big red star next to
all my spellings and
put a big gold star on
all my maths and tell my mum
I'm amazingly brilliant and
don't yell, "Did you bring that
horrible mouse to school again?"
when my mouse gets out of
my pocket and runs about.

It's not my fault!

Rules for my dog

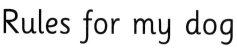

Don't sit under my chair when I'm eating my dinner and make smells. Everyone looks at me and says "Stop it!" and **it's not fair!**

Don't keep putting your wet nose in my pocket—my mouse doesn't like it.

Don't dig up Dad's best rose trees. I don't need you to help me find my worms.

Don't lick my knees.
It's horrible.
Go and lick my sister.

13

Rules for my mouse

Come when I call you and don't go round the back of the washing machine and stay there all night and don't wriggle about in my pocket and don't jump out and run around when my teacher's looking and please, please, please keep away from my mum.

You can play with my little sister.

15

Rules for EVERYONE EVERYWHERE

Be nice to me and my dog and my mouse.

Don't look at me when there's a smell in the room.

Don't give me horrible kisses. Give them to my little sister.

Don't pull a cross face when I show you my worm collection.

And when something horrible happens...

DON'T BLAME ME!

Twelve dancing princesses

a traditional tale by the Brothers Grimm

illustrated by Ilaria Matteini

Once there was a king who had twelve beautiful daughters.
They all slept in the same room, and every night the King made sure that they were safely locked in.

But every morning the princesses were tired and their shoes were all worn through.

"What do my daughters do each night?" asked the King. But no one knew.

At last the King announced that
anyone who could solve
the mystery could marry one of
the princesses.

Many princes tried, but not one
could keep awake long enough
to see.

One day a soldier made his way
to the palace. An old woman met
him and said, "The princesses are
under a magic spell. Don't drink
anything they bring you.
Just pretend to fall asleep."
Then she gave him a cloak.
"This will make you
invisible when you follow
the princesses."

That night, at the palace,
the eldest princess gave the soldier
some wine. He pretended to drink
it and then lay down as if he were
asleep.

At once the princesses got up and dressed in their finest clothes and jewels. Then they opened the door to a magic stairway. The soldier quickly put on his magic cloak and followed the princesses.

First they came to an enchanted woodland. The soldier broke off three shining branches and put them under his cloak.
"I'll show these to the King," he thought.

Then the princesses came to
a magnificent palace.
They danced there until
three o'clock in the morning.
At last they went home with their
shoes quite worn through.

The soldier hurried back too.

The next morning he showed
the King the three shining branches,
and told him everything
that had happened.

The King sent for his daughters
and asked them if the soldier was
telling the truth.
"Yes," they said sadly.
The princesses were sorry now that
they had deceived their father.

The soldier married the eldest princess,
and they all lived happily ever after.

The meeting

adapted from a poem by Derek Dwyer
illustrated by David Parkins

He was standing in our garden,
Looked at me and asked my name.
Told me once he used to live here,
But it didn't look the same.

He was glad we'd kept the apple tree.
He was happy now he'd been.
Said that I could tell my mum
I'd met a man called Sammy Green.

When I told my mum, her face went
    white;
She didn't say a lot.
I didn't ask her what was wrong,
I thought I'd better not.

But when I was in the graveyard,
I think I found out why.
I found the grave of Sammy Green...
And an apple tree nearby.

Learning to read with this book

Special features

My secret book of rules and other stories is ideal for early independent reading. It includes:

- two long, amusing stories planned to build stamina and encourage the possibilities of exciting writing.
- a traditional tale.
- an atmospheric rhyme to inspire imagination and aid memory and reading fluency.

Planned to help your child to develop her reading by:

- practising a variety of reading techniques such as recognising frequently used words on sight, being able to read words with similar spelling patterns (eg, been/green), and the use of letter-sound clues.

- using rhyme to improve memory.

- including illustrations that make reading even more enjoyable.

is specially designed to help your child learn to read. It will complement all the methods used in schools.

Parents took part in extensive research to ensure that **Read with Ladybird** would help your child to:

- take the first steps in reading
- improve early reading progress
- gain confidence in new-found abilities.

The research highlighted that the most important qualities in helping children to read were that:

- books should be fun – children have enough 'hard work' at school
- books should be colourful and exciting
- stories should be up to date and about everyday experiences
- repetition and rhyme are especially important in boosting a child's reading ability.

The stories and rhymes introduce the 100 words most frequently used in reading and writing.

These 100 key words actually make up half the words we use in speech and reading.

The three levels of **Read with Ladybird** consist of 22 books, taking your child from two words per page to 600-word stories.

Read with Ladybird will help your child to master the basic reading skills so vital in everyday life.

Ladybird have successfully published reading schemes and programmes for the last 50 years. Using this experience and the latest research, **Read with Ladybird** has been produced to give all children the head start they deserve.